positive social skills for teens

A Practical Guide for Teens to Boost Their Self-Confidence and Build Meaningful Connections for a Happy Life

Victoria Day

other guidance. If you require counseling, please get in touch with a qualified professional.

By reading this text, the reader accepts that the author will not be held liable for any damages, indirectly or directly, experienced due to the use of the information included herein, particularly, but not limited to, omissions, errors, or inaccuracies. As a reader, you are accountable for your decisions, actions, and consequences.

free gifts

To help you become an empowered teen in your journey to creating your dream life, I have created 3 FREE bonuses.

You can get instant access by signing up to my email newsletter below.

In addition to these 3 FREE resources, you will also be receiving free book giveaways in the future, discounts, and so much more.

To get your bonus, go to:
freebies.dreamworldpublications.com
Or Scan the QR code below

Positive Life Skills Worksheets

These are a set of worksheets that will help you keep organized and boost your productivity.

Inside, you will find:

- Goal Planner

- Weekly Morning Routine Checklist

- Weekly Planner

- Habit Tracker

- Expense Tracker

- And, more!

Magnetize: 23 Techniques for Teens to Boost their Social Skills and Charisma

Inside the book, you will discover a set of tips to boost your social skills. Some of these tips include:

- The broken record strategy

- Remembering names

- Learning to identify nonverbal cues

- Controlling your negative thoughts

- And many more!

Fight Your Fears: 10 Proven Strategies to Overcoming Worry and Anxiety

All of us struggle with fear and worry from time to time. Oftentimes, our fears limit our potential. Inside the book, you will gain a better understanding of fear and learn strategies to conquer it, you will learn:

• What is Fear?

• How to change your biology and control your thinking

• How to identify your fears

• Strategies to conquer fear

• How to get help

Get all of these resources for FREE by visiting the link below:

freebies.dreamworldpublications.com

contents

introduction

" We are social beings and our brains
grow in a social environment.

ERIC JENSEN

Did you know most Americans will encounter 10,000 people during their lifetime?[1] Now, that is a lot of people! Of course, you'll have many amazing experiences over the years as you meet these people, but you'll also have some bad ones. However, those bad encounters you might have won't be the death of your social life or self-esteem.

Take a deep breath—we're going to get through this together throughout this book.

Everyone has a few painfully embarrassing memories from our childhood and teenage years. Unfortunately, this is a time in your life when socializing can be particularly difficult. You are not alone in this; many of your peers have a hard time getting through this. This difficulty doesn't mean you shouldn't try—it merely shows how important it is to make friends right now.

You are still figuring out who you are and what you want to do with your life. So, this can often make you feel more pressured or stressed out trying to balance your friendships with everything else going on in your life.

If you are anxious, shy, or insecure around others, you might find it hard to talk to a new friend and make a great first impression. Or maybe you are lonely and isolated, and you do not get out as much as you want. If you are homeschooled, attend school online, or get depressed from time to time, this is understandable. Or maybe you only have a few casual acquaintances and wish you could have a closer friendship with them. Unfortunately, some teenagers experience all of the above feelings and situations.

Do you feel like you missed out on learning the unwritten social rules everyone else seems to know by thirteen? You are not alone, and it will get better.

It's easy to feel down when you compare yourself to your peers, who seem to breeze through life much easier than you. It's natural to wish you were one of them. You think it's impossible that they feel just as stuck in their heads as you do. However, even the most popular and happiest teenagers feel insecure and experience setbacks. They just hide it well.

You are not alone. Almost every teen in your school or neighborhood probably feels like you do. Of course, we're all unique in how we experience our lives, but one thing unites us:

we're all human and are doing the best we can to attain the life we want.

Do you know what we also have in common? We all crave connection as human beings.

This need for connections is nothing new. Our ancestors thrived by interacting with others over centuries. We did everything in social groups, whether hunting for meat, picking berries, or traveling on stagecoaches. But, aside from water, food, and safety, there are other things we need to make our lives feel complete. Maslow's Hierarchy of Needs, a psychological theory that illustrates what we need as humans, says we also need belonging and love. (See Figure 1.)[2] When these needs get met, our well-being increases, and we live a more fulfilling life.

Figure 1: Maslow's Hierarchy of Needs

I know what you feel because I was you. Though I did well in my classes as a teenager, I felt a knot in my stomach when it was time to make friends or just talk to someone. I would practice what I planned to say in my head and go over it repeatedly before talking to someone. However, I would mess up the conversation and stumble over my words. These social situations felt horrifying.

"How's school going?" someone would ask. It was an easy enough question, but my words used to get stuck in my throat whenever someone asked it. My brain would bombard me with my insecurities. I would have loved to talk about my achievements and the school subjects I loved, but I could only add the word "fine" to the conversation with my eyes stuck on the floor and rubbing my arms.

After many years of struggling socially, I hit a breaking point. Something had to change, I realized. What if I was the one keeping myself from moving ahead? Was it true that I was blocking my ability to be myself?

After asking myself these difficult questions and honestly answering them, I finally decided. My barrier was no longer keeping me safe from awkward social situations. It was a roadblock. So, I decided to do something about it. It was challenging and time-consuming, but I overcame all my obstacles with some hard work over time. And I know you can too!

As part of my self-healing process, I found many techniques that helped me strengthen my mental well-being and my social skills. As a result, I began to feel better as I continued my journey to improve my social life. Using these techniques made a big difference in my life, and I know they can help you make a significant change.

I put together this book based on the knowledge and experience that helped me improve my social skills and engage in meaningful relationships. This book is divided into four chapters. The first chapter of the book focuses on helping you understand and explore yourself, answering the important question of who you are. This exploration will help you see yourself clearly and make decisions that better represent who you are. The second chapter is all about building your confidence to portray yourself as you are without any masks or insecurities. The third chapter equips you with the skills you need to talk to your peers without feeling awkward. Finally, the fourth chapter is devoted to building meaningful relationships that will make your life more enjoyable.

Maybe you avoid going out and socializing because it feels too overwhelming. Or you avoid making acquaintances because you are afraid of making a mistake. Perhaps you feel anxious whenever the phone rings. Or maybe facing someone who has hurt you seems impossible. To put it mildly, it is all exhausting.

Whatever issues you face in your social life, this book will help you as it would have helped me when I was a teen. Keep turning the pages to brighten up your life.

one

the art of exploring yourself

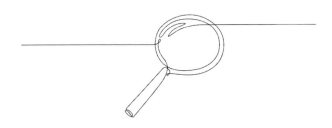

66 The most important things in life are the connections you make with others.

TOM FORD

YOUR PEERS likely come from different cultures and have their own ways of making friends and connecting with their classmates. As you've grown up over the years, those differences have probably influenced how you see the world and your community. These differences are a natural part of life, and they encourage healthy growth, both socially and mentally.

On the other hand, if our peers negatively influence us, it can affect our lives in unhealthy ways. For instance, if you make friends with someone who bullies you, that relationship can disrupt your others, often causing your other friends to abandon you. When this happens, it can negatively affect your mental health, lasting well into adulthood. So, as you can see, the social connections you make now can influence your life for many years to come.

When we experience social pain—through rejection or an insult— the sensation feels as real as physical pain. What does that mean? It means that things that cause us emotional pain affect our bodies as much as our minds. Because of the way we experience this stress, it makes it even more evident that a positive social life is a necessity rather than an option.

How about we explore this topic a little more?

1.1 Am I Born to Be Alone?

It's inevitable. All of us will face social difficulties throughout our lives. And this is never more present than in our teenage years. When this happens, you might think, *No one will ever understand me, so I am going to quit trying*, or *I am going to be alone forever*. However, our craving for connecting with our peers and making lasting memories with them tells us we are not doomed to feel alone forever.

Healthy relationships maximize our happiness and satisfaction because they remind us that our insecurities are not our reality. Here are some positive ways that enforce this idea in our lives:

- **Boosting Physical Health**

Having a strong social connection with one of your peers—feeling understood and bonded with them—can influence your health much more than obesity, smoking, or high blood pressure. Psychologist Sheldon Cohen, a professor at Carnegie Mellon University, led a research project in the 1990s that analyzed the effects of stress on our health. According to his research, college students who said they had great relationships found the chances reduced to half of catching a cold.[1]

Also, in 2018, an AARP study of adults over forty-five found that loneliness can also lead to poor health.[2] And these are things that don't simply happen overnight. Instead, isolation and loneliness might begin with emotional pain, then build over the years until you wake up one day to realize how lonely your life has been. That's why it's so important for you to build positive social skills now.

On the other end of the spectrum, having healthy friendships enhances your chances of being healthy. Researchers Fowler and Christakis found that non-obese people have higher chances of having non-obese friends because of how influential those healthy behaviors are in our relationships. This influence tends to spread throughout your social network and positively affects your emotional well-being and physical health.[3]

- **Extending Life Span**

Did you know you could longer just by having good friends? Although it may seem as if I'm making this up, social science research has actually shown it.[4] When you have friends who are supportive and there for you on good and bad days, you feel good inside. Positive emotions reduce stress responses, causing fewer health problems and extending your life.

- **Reducing Stress**

Can you think of something that relieves the pressure when you feel stressed out? One way is to lean on your friends for support. Even if all they can do is listen to what's going on in your life, it can help lighten the weight of the world when it becomes too much to bear.

- **Boosting Mental Health**

Healthy friendships can improve your mental health, giving you feelings of belonging, purpose, enjoyment, stress reduction, and improved self-worth and confidence. Likewise, you might be prone to anxiety, depression, and other mental health disorders without these relationships throughout your life.

- **Boosting Happiness**

When you spend more time with friends who genuinely care for you, you will feel less lonely. And over time, these friendships will contribute to an overall boost in happiness that will leave a lasting influence on your teenage years, often even extending into adulthood.

- **Fulfilling a Sense of Purpose**

Many of your peers want to feel like they are helping others and making the world a better place in some way. Having meaningful friendships can give you a sense of fulfillment and purpose, especially when you experience the positive difference you make in their lives.

On the other hand, not forming bonds with others can lead to many health problems, including:

- **Depression**

Extended periods of loneliness can lead to depression, which can have a range of negative effects on your life. When you're depressed, you tend to withdraw from your friends and family even more. Your education, hygiene, and other relationships can also suffer. Noticing the signs now will help you prepare better for a healthier future.

- **High Blood Pressure**

The University of Chicago conducted a study in 2010 that found a direct relationship between long periods of loneliness and high blood pressure.[5] While these long-term effects which can lead to heart problems down the road—take some time to show up, the social skills and habits you build today will help you prevent those problems later.

- **Weak Immune System**

Earlier in this chapter, I talked about how positive friendships can help boost your immune system, but the opposite is also true. A lack of a positive social experience in your teenage years can weaken your immune system, causing you to catch more colds and other viruses more easily than your peers.

With all these advantages and disadvantages hanging over your head, it makes it even more critical to understand how to develop your best social life now so you can reap the benefits in the future. To do that, it all starts with how well you understand who you are and what you want out of life.

1.2 Who am I?

This time in your life is one of exploration and discovery as you learn about the things you love, the people you like to spend time with, the activities you like to do, and what mark you want to leave on the world. It's important not to ignore how significant these things are because they will be with you for the rest of your life. But if you don't understand what they are now, something else could also follow you for the rest of your life: a lack of confidence in who you are and what you can accomplish.

Another positive benefit of getting to know yourself is that it will help you connect better with your classmates and friends. This improved connection is possible because it helps you build a foundation that allows you to connect with others. Without that foundation, you can't build lasting relationships that make you feel like you've made meaningful connections with others.

When you do not make an effort to explore who you are, your awareness of individuality fades. As a result, you get easily pressured into doing things you wouldn't normally do. However, I have some good news for you: you can slowly build the life you want by checking in with yourself regularly. The better you know yourself, the better you can live your life.

So, let's start.

- **Start Journaling**

You will be giving a playground for all the connected thoughts and ideas in your head, whether you spend ten minutes, half an hour, or more writing your daily journal entry.

Journaling will help you become more aware of such thoughts by providing them with a place to play. You instruct your brain to pay attention by writing things down, and it will pay more attention to those thoughts you tell it are important. Eventually, you'll start confessing things you had only half-consciously entertained before.

We lie to ourselves more often than we would like to admit. Sometimes we convince ourselves we made bad decisions for good or rational reasons, even if we were simply angry or lazy. However, avoiding the true motivations behind our actions does not help us grow or understand who we are. Remember that lying to yourself is pointless. Even if you find out things about yourself you do not like, this provides you the opportunity to confront those issues rather than pretending they don't exist.

- **Evaluate Your Strength and Weaknesses**

By writing down your strengths and weaknesses, you paint a better picture of who you are and what matters most to you. You should also consider what your friends, family, and classmates think about your strengths and weaknesses. These are the things others notice about you, and they can give you some excellent insight into how you see your place in the world around you.

Determination, commitment, self-discipline, thinking, patience, decisiveness, diplomacy, communication skills, and imagination or creativity are examples of strengths.

Close-mindedness, self-centeredness, difficulties recognizing reality, judging others, and control issues are all examples of flaws.

During your evaluation, it's important not to internalize your perceived weaknesses too much. Just because you're not as strong with these things, it doesn't mean you are a failure or something is wrong with you. Instead, it simply shows you the areas in your life that have room to grow.

- **Figure Out Your Values**

Your values will guide you through life. Understanding your values is an excellent place to start when you want to understand yourself better. They will help you prioritize what's important to you and teach you how to say "no" to things that force you to stray from those values. Here's an exercise for you.

Living by Values

Write everything important to you on sticky notes. The list is about what you value in the things or relationships that are important to you, not about people (names) or things themselves (cars, houses, etc.). Friendship, comfort, patience, and integrity are good examples of positive values to focus on in this exercise.

If you find this exercise challenging or confusing, here are some self-reflection questions that can guide your journaling:

- Write down all the times in your life when you were happy.
- What were you doing during those times?
- What were your feelings at the time? Why?
- Think about times when you felt proud or fulfilled.
- What made you feel proud or satisfied?
- What drives your desire to be fulfilled?
- Think about times when you had to make tough choices.
- What was the issue?
- What made you frightened?
- What difficulties did you have to face?
- How did it feel to make the right choice?

Go over everything you wrote. As you go over the list, consider different values that come to mind. Make a list of those values.

- Make a list of ten values. Remove the least significant ones from the list if you have more than ten.
- Make the list shorter. Give yourself thirty seconds to delete three values from the equation. Which are the insignificant ones? Which values can you let go of without losing your sense of self?
- You have 30 seconds left to remove two more values.
- This is your last chance to focus on what really matters to you. Allow another 30 seconds to remove two more values. Which ones will you delete?
- At the end of this step, only three values should remain. Your fundamental values are the ideas that are most important to you.
- Read your list aloud to yourself. Tell a friend about it.
- How do you feel about it?
- What values are missing?

- How will you live up to those values?
- How have you previously betrayed these principles?
- What would you change the next time?

- **Realize Your Priorities**

What is most valuable to you can reveal a great deal about yourself. Consider your priorities, how they compare to the priorities of other people you respect, and what your conclusions reveal about you. Of course, you must open yourself to the possibility that your priorities are out of order (as many people are), which can teach you a lot about yourself.

What would you do if your room or house caught fire? Make a list of the things you would save. It is incredible how fire reveals our priorities. Even if you save something useful, such as your schoolbooks, it says something about you (maybe that you value your education and your future).

Another way to figure out your priorities is to imagine someone you care about is being openly criticized for something you disagree with (for example, they want to get a pet tarantula, but you are deathly afraid of spiders). Do you agree with them? Protect them? How? What are your thoughts? When faced with being criticized by our friends, our actions can reveal our priorities.

Money, friendship, family, respect, stability, security, material possessions, and comfort are some examples of priorities most of us value.

- **Notice How You Respond When You're Emotional**

You might become extremely angry, depressed, joyful, or thrilled at times. Understanding what triggers these stronger-than-normal reactions, as well as the main cause, can help you gain a deeper understanding of yourself.

For example, perhaps you become quite enraged when others talk during a movie. Are you furious because of the talking or because you believe it was a personal sign of disrespect? Because your rage isn't helping the problem, you could be better off focusing on calming techniques to distract from your intense emotions. Breathing or meditating, for example, might help you through this situation.

- **Understand What Makes You Happy**

Take some time to think about what matters to you—and why. Psychologist Ginger Houghton recommends imagining your ideal day to explore what matters most to you. This perfect day could be something that happened in the past or something you want to happen in the future.[6]

Imagine your perfect day from sunrise to bedtime, as Houghton suggests:

- How do you feel when you wake up first thing in the morning?
- What do you do throughout the day?
- What are you seeing?
- What do you taste, smell, and hear?
- How does your day make you feel?
- Reflect on your day before going to bed —how do you feel?
- Why did today make you happy?

- **Find What Resonates with You**

Consider the books, movies, and television series that emotionally impact you. Then look at why you identify so strongly with these things.

- **Find What Drains or Energizes You**

Houghton also recommends making two lists to help you use your self-awareness to create better days:

One list should have activities and people that recharge you and make you feel like your best self, while the other contains activities and people that drain or deplete you.

Is it weighing you down to overcommit to activities and people-pleasing?

Houghton suggests revisiting these lists in a few days. You can talk to a friend or a family member who knows you well to figure out the patterns in your lists.[7]

- **Write Your Biography**

In twenty minutes, write a 500-word biography. This activity will encourage you to type quickly and think less about what to include in your life story, which will help you identify what your brain thinks influences who you are. Though you might not type 500 words in such a short amount of time, this activity can reveal a lot about yourself through what you're disappointed you didn't include in your biography.

- **Try a Writing Exercise**

When writers sit down to write a book, they use various techniques when creating fictional characters for their story. You can use the same exercises to learn more about yourself, and many of them are available for free online. These exercises may not have anything concrete to say about you, but you can discover that on your own with some critical thinking. To try this for yourself, you can answer the following questions:

- In one sentence, how would you define yourself?
- What is your role in the story of your life?
- What was the most significant event in your life? What effect did it have on you?
- What makes you different from your friends or family members?

- **Identify Your Toxic Behaviors**

Even the most positive people can engage in toxic behaviors or patterns without realizing it. Here is how to detect if you engage in toxic behaviors, what it means, and how to change those negative habits.

- **Always Sarcastic**

People who only see negativity in a situation can be exhausting to be around in the long run. Even when done to make someone laugh, teasing can quickly turn into hatred. We have all experienced the pain of being the subject of such insults, especially when we feel vulnerable. So, before you say anything, think to yourself, *How would I feel if someone responded in this way to me?* It's likely it wouldn't make you feel very good, so it's best to avoid making sarcastic remarks.

- **Competing in Everything**

Telling someone you had a similar experience to them is not the same as talking about how you have had it worse. The first allows you to show empathy, and the second comes off as competing with your friend. Consider why you feel compelled to compete—is it because it is the only way to feel recognized or get some relief from your pain or challenges? If you have trouble expressing compassion for others, consider asking yourself, "What would I want someone to say to me in my situation?"

- **Wanting to Fix Everything**

Some of us are born rescuers and fixers—perhaps you have been taught to handle difficult situations, or maybe you seek out such friendships without realizing it. Perhaps you simply enjoy providing solutions. However, this is emotional labor, and as the job mounts up, so do your frustrations and resentments. Simply put, other people's projects are not ours. Just because we can solve a problem does not mean we should—the obligation lies firmly with the other person, who might not even recognize the situation as an issue.

- **Always Playing the Role of the Victim**

Because of the care you receive from traumatic events, some people subconsciously crave it. When we want to change, we usually have two opposing sides. One side wants to change, while the other does not since it gives them the added benefit of attention or special treatment because of our trauma. As much as we might not want to admit it, a part of us may like the attention that comes with the drama and the resulting pity parties.

If you find yourself playing the role of the victim often, you probably don't realize you're doing it. You can change this behavior by detaching yourself from the drama and figuring out what you need to do to let go of it completely. If it's a serious situation, such as bullying or getting into a fight at school, it could help to talk to a trusted adult about what happened. They can help you figure out the best way to let go of the pain you're feeling.

- **Pointing Out Everybody's Flaws**

One of the most embarrassing things as a teenager is when someone points out your flaws. Likewise, if you do this to others, it makes them feel humiliated, and it might also deeply hurt their feelings. If you need to say something, you could try this conversation starter: "I've observed this difference in you, and I am here if you ever want to talk." Then hand the ball on to them. Do this privately to lessen the embarrassment or any hurt feelings.

- **Forcing Your Solutions**

We want to shout it from the mountain-tops when we find a solution, especially after being stuck for a long period. Whether it is about your religious beliefs or staying fit, we hope our loved ones will benefit from it. Keep in mind that you are their loved one, not their doctor or coach, and your job is not to treat or save them. You can set the best example for them by living your life without telling them how to live theirs. You can gently open the conversation when they are ready to ask for your advice.

I hope these suggestions will help you get a clear picture of who you are and what kind of people you want to associate with in life. They will also help you focus on your negative traits and eliminate them. In the next chapter, we will discuss how you can develop self-confidence to thrive better in social situations.

Chapter Takeaway:

- You, as a human, need and deserve social connections.
- Social interaction makes you happy and satisfied with life.
- Know yourself better so you can portray that clear image to others and attract people like you.

two

the art of being confident

" Self-confidence can be learned, practiced, and mastered—just like any other skill. Once you master it, everything in your life will change for the better.

BARRIE DAVENPORT

IN SOCIAL SITUATIONS, it might be challenging to feel confident. In reality, most people experience some anxiety when socializing with their peers. This difficulty is normal. The fear and exhilaration alter your brain chemistry. When you anticipate a fun or frightening event, dopamine and adrenaline are released in a rush. This release can help you feel more secure about the upcoming social event if you understand this is a biological process practically everyone experiences.

Do you want to feel more confident in social situations? Here are some techniques for overcoming fear and confidently approaching others in social situations. *This is fantastic,* you might think, *but what if I am in the situation and do not feel confident?* It is okay if you experience a flood of unpleasant emotions or find yourself in a new setting feeling anxious or uncertain. It takes time to build confidence in social situations; however, gaining confidence becomes easier with practice. This chapter will discuss some of the best ways to boost your inner and outer social confidence and challenge the feeling that you do not belong.

2.1 Shy Away from Awkwardness

Are you the person who sits in the corner of the party, hoping no one will approach you? If the answer is yes, know that you are not alone. You must adopt a confident attitude and practice developing your social skills if you want to become more socially confident. At your next party, you might be the one who approaches the wallflower.

Here are some tips for you:

- **Accept Your Personality**

Many people are introverts, which means they prefer to spend their time alone with their thoughts. If this describes you, do not try to become an outgoing, social person overnight. Trying to force this change causes anxiety, tension, and even health issues. Instead, spend time with people you already like and aim to make the best of your time together. This strategy will give you more meaningful memories to treasure when you're older.

Accepting your introverted personality allows you to concentrate on the quality of your social interactions rather than striving to improve the number of interactions. That old saying is true: Quality is more important than quantity.

- **Understand Why You Need Confidence**

By interacting with your peers, you can improve your confidence in your social skills. These abilities are known as social competence. This is just a fancy term for understanding how to act in a social situation. Even if you don't have those skills now, you can get better by practicing them, which will give you more opportunities to make friends and stop the loneliness from creeping into your life.

How do you see yourself in social situations? When we're not confident, we believe we're making a bad first impression, but that isn't always the case. You're probably simply trying to acknowledge how hard it is when you find yourself in a social situation.

- **Prepare Yourself**

Building a strategy to "survive" a social event might help you if you suffer from shyness or social anxiety. You will feel more confident in your surroundings since you know what to expect. While this might not be possible for every social event you attend, it is possible for many, and it might give you some peace of mind. For instance, if your friend is having a birthday party, you could ask her ahead of time who she invited and what games or activities she has planned for the party. This preparation helps you process what is about to happen. Knowing specifics might help you relax, especially if you are detail-oriented. Getting this information from your friend can help you feel more confident when you step through that door.

- **Don't Let Negative Thoughts Impact You**

If you don't feel confident in social situations, it's easy to look for proof that validates your belief. However, what harm would it do to imagine proving yourself wrong? If you walk into a friend's party feeling confident you'll have the time of your life, that positive shift in your belief about yourself will boost your confidence. So, whenever you catch yourself thinking negative thoughts, ask yourself why the opposite can't be true.

Consider this: you are out, and you think to yourself, *I know everyone here thinks I'm dull because I have nothing interesting to say.* Stop this thought in its tracks and picture yourself engaged in several interesting conversations with your peers.

- **Put Your Beliefs to the Test**

Once you validate your feelings, you can look at the situation to see if the result was outside your control. Don't take responsibility for others' reactions, as this can cause you more anxiety. Instead, recognize that these reactions are because of something they did or felt, not something you caused. It will also help if you show them compassion for whatever is going on in their lives that makes them react this way.

Perhaps you misunderstood a facial expression, thinking they were uninterested in what you said, or maybe someone ended a conversation and left without explaining themselves. It's unhealthy to assume these reactions are your fault. Maybe your peer was not feeling well or saw someone they didn't want to see. They could have also been late getting home for dinner and didn't want to get in trouble. It's also possible your friend felt some social anxiety and needed a moment alone to breathe through the stress.

As you can see, the possibilities are endless that explain why someone acted a certain way. If you feel bad about something similar, you can take a moment to think through what happened and show empathy for others.

- **Expect the Unexpected**

Sometimes social situations are unpredictable, and the unexpected can happen. An unexpected experience at a social event can quickly drive you out of your comfort zone. If you walk into any social situation realizing the unexpected can happen, you will have a much easier time. Take a deep breath and accept that you will not be able to control every social interaction. Consider all the positive social encounters you have had that were unexpected. This exploration can help build your confidence and show you how to handle social situations with ease.

- **Be Mindful of Your Body Language**

Your body language communicates your emotions to those around you. Whether you realize it or not, your body communicates how you feel naturally. Likewise, your peers might not realize their paying attention to what your body language says, but it's hard to ignore when socializing in person.

Your body normally produces chemicals that make you feel the way you believe you should. When you are in a stressful situation, your body assumes you're in danger. Your body will create high levels of cortisol, adrenaline, and other chemicals to prepare for your fight or flight reaction. This hormonal increase is harmless in tiny amounts. However, being constantly anxious can negatively affect your health.

Even when you're not in a stressful environment, you might react as though you feel stressed if you usually experience social anxiety in these situations. This reaction will show in your body language. This type of body language can appear when you try to take up less space, avoid eye contact, or speak rapidly to avoid being interrupted.

On the other hand, if you feel secure in your social skills, you won't act as though you feel you're in danger. Instead, you will feel calm and at ease. The hormones your body produces express this naturally, and your peers will see how confident you are as a result.

Just like a stress response presents itself on your body in a certain way, so does your confidence. Because you feel safe, you will stand and sit with great posture, raise your hands above your head, moderate your movements, and take other confident poses.

By displaying your confidence through body language, you believe you can overcome social anxiety. However, correcting your body language is only the beginning. You should also work on your mental health to address any issues causing your social anxiety.

- **Be Mindful of Your Tone of Voice**

Keep your tone of voice in mind. In any conversation you have with your peers, especially an uncomfortable one, a friendly or soothing tone of voice will make the person you're talking to feel safe. You will also feel more secure if you are aware of how you phrase things. If your voice is calm and kind, you put others at ease. Avoid sarcasm; it can confuse your friends and classmates and make you feel insecure if they do not get that you're joking with them. If you want others to hear you, try to talk clearly, not louder, but slower, and avoid sounding aggressive. Practice talking about something in front of a mirror and pay attention to how you say it and how you perceive your tone of voice.

- **Remember Who You Are and What You Value**

Being honest about who you are and what you value in life is essential for building your confidence. Do you think you can be confident if you are not yourself? "The Ultimate Guide to Confidence" on Hubspot has a lot to say on this topic: "Confidence boosts our self-esteem, reduces stress, and often drives us to act."[1] So, how can you be content when faced with social situations if your confidence is low? Going into a potentially embarrassing situation by accepting who you are. When you feel nervous or insecure, your words or behavior might come off as fake or forced.

Try some self-reflection if you are not sure what you value. This internal exploration might include anything from journaling to going on a long walk at the park alone. First, get to know who you are and what you enjoy and dislike. After that, you can evaluate your values. Many people find that being comfortable with themselves gives them the confidence to engage others during social situations. So, if you have not already, make sure to do so.

- **Slowly Move Out of Your Comfort Zone**

You might have heard that the most effective way to gain social confidence is to put yourself in situations that are miles away from your comfort zone, like approaching strangers and introducing yourself. This strategy, however, does not work for most people because it is not long-term.

Instead, build your confidence by taking tiny steps forward. First, make a note of the social settings that make you feel uncomfortable. Sort them from the least to the most frightening. Then, working your way through the list, begin with the easiest challenge.

For instance, your list might look something like this:

- Make eye contact with someone I do not know.
- Smile at the cashier.
- Say "Good morning" to a classmate.

While waiting for the bus after school, strike up a conversation with a peer you haven't met yet.

You will become less bashful and more socially confident with practice. Socializing will feel less forced and more natural.

If you are an introvert who finds socializing exhausting, you can find ways to boost your social stamina. You might also find my advice on becoming more extroverted without sacrificing your identity useful.

- **Show Interest and Listen Actively**

Make others feel welcome, important, and heard. Pay attention to the verbal and nonverbal cues you send to others. These active listening skills will help you recognize ways to improve your social skills.

For example, maybe you noticed that avoiding eye contact and crossing your arms at social gatherings makes other people uncomfortable.

You need to concentrate on what the other person is saying and attempt to picture yourself in the situation. This focus can help you show more empathy toward your peers, allowing you to respond thoughtfully to keep the conversation going. Letting the other person speak can remind you that you are not responsible for the entire conversation. It also says to others that you value and care about their thoughts, resulting in more significant relationships with your peers and increased self-confidence.

When you are nervous, it is tempting to focus on yourself, how nervous you are, and how you will react. However, this could give the impression that you are uninterested in what they have to say.

Avoid interrupting, which you may feel compelled to do if you are nervous. Instead, pause and wait until the other person has finished their sentence before responding.

- **Be Intentional in Your Interactions**

Being deliberate can make you feel as if you did everything you could to take a step toward becoming more social. Accomplishment can boost your confidence, and knowing you were deliberate at the end of the day can provide you with a sense of security and contentment. So, try to become more at ease in social situations. For example, you could try going to the mall alone or making plans to eat lunch with a new friend from your favorite class. Intentional actions should benefit you, no matter what it is.

- **Practice Self-Amusement**

It is difficult to express yourself when you are constantly scared of rejection. Instead of communicating your true feelings or sense of humor, you might feel more at ease making statements you believe your peers will accept.

Funny people are usually highly confident. Most of the time, they don't filter what they say. Instead, they come up with a clever remark, and it appears effortless.

Everyone has this filter. Even the most self-assured of your classmates recognize that some things are best left unsaid. Filtering your thoughts is simply the courteous thing to do. On the other hand, an anxious person has an extremely sensitive filter. Fear of rejection causes them to hold back far too much.

You can adjust the sensitivity level of that filter now that you have overcome nervousness and are spending time with more confident people. It is finally time to start laughing at yourself and saying exactly what you want without worrying about what other people might think of you.

- **Think of a Role Model**

Without spending too much time on this, what role model comes to mind first? As you think about this person, answer the following questions:

- What topics does this person like to discuss?
- What is their posture like? What does their body language show about them?
- What is their energy level?

If you observe a group of socially confident people, you will notice that they are not all alike. Some people, for example, are calm and wonderful listeners. Others are outgoing and charismatic, and their sense of humor draws people to them naturally. People with social skills know how to let their personalities shine while making others feel at ease. You will develop your social style with practice.

These are some general suggestions that will help you develop the confidence you need to interact with people and be yourself. Below I have given some specific tips for you if you feel too often that you do not belong or feel alien among other people.

2.2 I Do Not Belong

"I always feel like I'm on the outside looking in, as if no one understands or cares about me. I am always feeling like I'm on the B team. I am a side option."

Do you feel like an outsider in social situations? Even if you all are doing the same activity somehow, you feel different. No matter what you do, you feel like you do not belong. It is called the outsider syndrome. It can be your belief, you might have values and opinions different from others, or you might try to fit in the wrong group. Let's explore what you can do about that.

- **You Are Not Alone**

Most of us experience feeling like an outsider at some point.

Consider moments when you were an outsider who was eventually welcomed and included in a community. Recalling these memories might make it simpler for you to believe you will be accepted again.

It is easy to assume everyone else in your group feels the same way you do when you are an outsider. Try opening conversations about how others feel like outsiders if you can. For example, you could say, "I was reading that many famous people, even ones you would not think, felt like outsiders. Albert Einstein, Leonardo DiCaprio, and Rihanna were among the names on the list I saw. What are your thoughts? Do you believe that everyone feels that way at some point? Is this one of the reasons they were so motivated?"

This allows people to talk about their personal experiences without making themselves feel vulnerable.

- **Practice Daily**

If you have trouble forming close friendships in one-on-one or group situations, you should concentrate on your social skills. Spending some time strengthening your ability to make small talk, form friendships, and overcome discomfort can help you feel confident in your ability to be liked by people.

At least ten minutes per day should be spent learning more about social skills, and ten minutes should be spent practicing those skills. Consider making a reading list of articles that might help you and using what you learned in those articles to set daily goals for yourself. For example, you might set a goal to greet a different neighbor each day of the week, or you could pick someone new to study for an exam with once a week. Easing into a social situation like this will help you practice your social skills one-on-one before stepping into a group situation.

- **Start by Getting to Know One Person in a Group**

It might be difficult to feel a sense of belonging in a group. Break it down by creating deeper one-on-one relationships with others you know a little better. This method can be used at school, with friends after school, or within your family.

Choose your favorite three (or so) persons from your group and make a determined effort to learn more about them. Invite them to occasions where there will only be the two of you, such as watching a movie or going to the library to check out an interesting book you'll read and discuss together.

Concentrate on becoming closer friends with those three people. To become close buddies, you'll need to open up to them and allow them to see the real you. Knowing each person in the group individually might help you feel more accepted and involved in the group as a whole.

You might already feel less of an outcast in the group once you feel safe that these people know and accept you. If not, choose more people and devote more time to getting to know them.

- **Respect Other's Values and Expect
  the Same**

When our opinions and values differ from those around us, we can easily feel like outsiders. These disagreements are especially tough when dealing with close relatives.

You might feel inclined to conceal your opposing opinions to fit in. Hiding your true feelings might work for a little while, but you are more likely to feel even more alienated. "They just like me because they don't know the real me," you might assume.

It is still possible to feel included if your values are different. Everyone should respect each other's beliefs. Make it clear you respect their beliefs, and you want them to respect yours.

Try saying, "I know we feel differently about that, but I think we can all agree that . . ." the next time your values make you feel like an outsider.

If I'm with my family, for example, I might say:

"I understand we disagree on the finer points of politics, but I believe we can all agree that politicians must work together to get the best results for everyone."

- **Solve Isolating Issues**

Some issues, such as language or cultural barriers, can make you feel lonely and alone. If this contributes to your isolation, think about how to address the issue directly.

Many language classes also include cultural guidelines. They can also provide you with a sense of belonging in the class, as other students are likely to experience similar problems.

Other practical issues include being too far away from your social circle or not having enough money to go out. If this is a challenge you have, perhaps you might need to skip a social event or two, but hopefully, you can still participate when you have enough money to participate once a month or once every other week.

If in doubt, discuss some solutions with your social group. If you are unsure how to bring it up, you can say, "I would love to spend more time with you guys, but living so far away makes it tough. Here is what I think could help. Do you think that would work?"

"My knee problem is acting up, so I won't be able to go to the gym this week. But what if I host a board game night?"

"I'm afraid I can't afford to eat out this week. Is it possible to play football in the park?"

- **Change Your Self-Talk**

The inability to trust that other people want you around can make you feel like an outsider. Improving your self-esteem and confidence takes time, but each step gets you closer to the social life you want.

It is difficult to build self-confidence while looking on the outside. Isolation can quickly become a source of self-criticism when you engage in negative self-talk.

Concentrate on what you tell yourself. When you discover yourself engaging in negative self-talk, try not to become annoyed or angry. Instead, try to fix your negative self-talk before moving on. For instance, if you tell yourself:

"No one wants to see me. "I'm worthless."

Stop and say something like this to yourself:

"I know how it feels, and it hurts. However, this is not the case. People want me around because I'm a kind and caring friend. I'm only now beginning to believe it."

• Do Not Push for Acceptance

You can come across as clingy if you try too hard to fit in with your social group. Ironically, accepting your lack of inclusion can help fix the problem of feeling like an outsider. You become more appealing to others to want to be around because you don't come across as needy.

For example, if you are talking with a group of friends and can't seem to get a word edgewise, rather than trying everything to get attention, be okay with not being part of the conversation for a while. However, if you want to add to the conversation, do so because you believe it will be useful, not because you want attention.

Remember to choose the right people. When you are with the right people, you can feel it in your gut. They encourage you, make your heart sing, and inspire you to feel your best. It is difficult to leave a group of people that isn't right for you, but I assure you it will feel better after you do.

The next chapter is about having great conversations with your peers.

Chapter Takeaway:

- Stay grounded in your values, beliefs, and sense of self.
- Be mindful of your body language and voice tone and learn to listen actively.
- Start small and understand that learning social skills takes time.
- Find your right group and do not push for acceptance.
- Look for solutions for your isolation and keep a positive attitude.

three
the art of
mastering a
conversation

“ Communication – the human
connection – is the key to personal
and career success.

PAUL J. MEYER

WHAT MEANING pops in your head when I
say "communication?" Of course, most of us

would say it is about words.

What if I tell you that more than half of what you say is irrelevant if your facial expressions do not align with your words?

Communication is a lot more than just words.

This chapter will focus on communication skills that are essential to form and maintain friendships and establish a strong social support system. Let's start with the basics, then move forward with more detailed ones later.

3.1 The ABCs of Communication

Perhaps the most crucial life skill is the ability to communicate effectively. It helps us connect with others and comprehend what our peers say to us. To appreciate how important communication is, just watch a baby listening carefully to their mother and trying to replicate the sounds she makes.

Effective communication is not only about the exchange of information, but it's also about understanding the motivation and emotion behind what you say. You must clearly deliver a message and listen to understand the meaning of the message. You should also ensure the other person feels understood and heard.

Since we seem to communicate with people every day, it feels like it's something we should naturally know how to do well. A conversation, however, frequently goes wrong. We say something, but the person we're talking to understands it differently. This miscommunication causes confusion, conflict, and hurt feelings at school and home.

In the previous chapter, we discussed active listening, body language, and tone of voice. Let's discuss a bit of active listening in detail, along with other communication skills.

- **Hearing vs. Listening**

The distinction between listening and hearing is significant, even though they sound like the same thing on the surface. You can hear minor changes in someone's voice that tell you how they feel and the emotions conveyed when you really listen—when you engage with what they say. When you listen actively, you not only gain a better understanding of the other person, but you also make them feel understood, which can help you form a stronger, deeper bond.

Listening actively and attentively will feel easy if you genuinely want to understand and connect with your peers. If not, try the following suggestions:

- Concentrate entirely on the person speaking. If you continuously check your phone or think about something else, you can't listen attentively. To pick up on small subtleties and vital nonverbal indications in a discussion, you must stay in the present moment. If some people are difficult to focus on, try repeating their words in your brain to emphasize their point and keep you engaged.
- Favor your right ear. The key processing regions for speech comprehension and emotions are located on the left side of the brain, which may sound strange. However, because the left part of the brain is linked to the right side of the body, favoring your right ear can assist you in perceiving emotional nuances in a conversation.

- **Avoid Judgment**

It is important to keep a cheerful attitude and an open mind when you attempt to help a friend, neighbor, or classmate. Use the following tips to become a non-judgmental listener:

- **Assess Your Mental State**

Before talking to someone about your issues, be mindful that you are in the right headspace to chat and listen without passing judgment. Analyze your state of mind to see if you are open, calm, and ready to help your friend in need.

- **Focus on Acceptance, Authenticity, and Empathy**

Acceptance is when you recognize someone's feelings, personal values, and experiences as fair, even if they deviate from yours or you disagree with them. Imagining yourself in the other person's shoes helps you build compassion and sincerity.

- **Focus on Verbal Skills**

Simple language skills can show you are paying attention. For example, asking questions, looking for nonverbal clues, listening to tone of voice, and not interrupting the person gives your peers room to express their thoughts and feelings.

- **Maintain Positive Body Language**

Your body language can demonstrate that you are paying attention and actually care. For example, you can try sitting instead of standing and maintaining comfortable eye contact with an open body position.

- **Express Yourself Clearly**

When you communicate with your peers, your main goal is to express yourself. It is about being honest and upfront with others about your views and feelings. You can also assert yourself, which means you can stand up for your convictions while also respecting the opinions of others.

Being assertive does not imply being aggressive or demanding. It is about honoring yourself, your needs, and your values. There is a right and a wrong time to give someone a firm "no." You'll also learn how to phrase anything unpleasant in a positive way and how to deal with criticism of any kind.

- **Set Aside Your Ego**

Your peers would not like it if you spoke or wrote about something as though only you know everything. People don't want to feel like you think they are beneath you simply because your opinions differ. There is room for inclusion when you communicate positively.

Every conversation should begin with the assumption that you have something to learn. Sometimes that means putting your personal feelings of pride aside.

Because we are all only human, it is all too easy to come off as arrogant and superior in conversation. Try pausing before speaking and noticing if you project too much of your emotions into this issue to keep yourself in check. Do you have feelings of insecurity? Do you feel threatened, defensive, or hurt? Recognizing that we boost our egos because of our internal worries and insecurities can be the first step toward better communication.

- **Avoid Short Answers**

Are you someone who answers all questions with the fewest words possible if you can get away with it?

Even the best conversationalists struggle to keep a conversation going when you only give them one-word answers!

Question: "Do you have a favorite film?" Answer: "*Star Wars.*"

Question: "Do you have any interests?" Answer: "Hiking."

These responses will not work.

Instead, aim for two-sentence responses as a rule of thumb.

"*Star Wars* is my favorite film. This film has hugely influenced my life, and I still aspire to be a Jedi!"

"I enjoy hiking. It helps me unwind, enjoy the scenery, and get some good exercise at the same time!"

Answer the question first, then explain why. You are not only answering their question, but you are also giving them a window into your world.

You might surprise yourself by discovering more about who you are once you start answering questions in this way!

What is it about your favorite dish that you enjoy?

And what is it about your favorite music that you find so appealing?

- **Go with the Flow**

When you think about what to say next, it is simple to stop listening. Consider "listening" like a dam that holds water. We keep the flow dammed up when we stop listening to think about what we are going to say next. As soon as those ideas enter your mind, let them out, then return to the conversation.

- **Manage Your Emotions**

We almost always allow our emotions to lead us into a conversation much too often when we talk about a sensitive issue. We then lose sight of the real purpose of the conversation. This emotional reaction can result in an unpleasant circumstance where we say things we regret later.

Strong emotions like love and stress can easily cloud our judgment and prevent us from thinking rationally during social interactions. Emotional intelligence skills can help us return to a sensible and relaxed state in these situations, allowing us to interact with others without losing our cool.

- **Clarify What You Heard**

We all bring biases to our discussions. These factors influence how we communicate and how we understand what others say. There are so many possibilities for misinterpretation! Ask for clarification to be safe rather than apologizing. Say, "I simply want to make sure I understand you correctly." This clarification can make a big difference in a meaningful conversation with a friend or a heated discussion with a family member. Double-checking will save you from misunderstandings.

- **Use Manners**

Manners are essential. If you do not want others to take you for granted, treat everyone with respect. From your best friend to your brother or sister, manners are the social contract we must all follow to remain civilized. Say thank you, please, and excuse me; be considerate of others, including their time; communicate with eye contact; avoid distractions (including technology) when speaking with others.

We must pay attention to minor details like gestures and visuals while communicating with one another because communication is not only about words. Actually, communication is a complicated process that requires our full attention and respect to express what we think and feel.

Let's get into the specifics of a conversation.

3.2 My Conversation Skills

Does the thought of a boring talk with Uncle Bob fill you with anxiety? If you are like most individuals, the anticipation of a conversation causes a few beads of sweat to form on your brow.

But here is the good news: when we make it easier on ourselves, we can learn social skills and have a lot of fun at the same time. Are you ready?

- **Find Common Ground**

Finding what you have in common is one of the easiest ways to start bonding with someone new. If there is a chance to develop a strong connection with someone, that is always a wonderful experience.

Be careful, however, because arguments can arise if you do not already know where a person stands on issues like politics, religion, or other divisive topics. Therefore, you should avoid topics like that if you want to avoid potential arguments. Taking the risk to talk about these difficult subjects, on the other hand, could pay off if you discover you have more in common than not.

- **Change a Question into a Statement**

"This feels like an interview." Has someone ever said this to you in a conversation? I've heard this several times in my life.

I was intrigued by the other person and wanted to learn more about her life. However, it is also understandable that she felt like she was being probed!

Instead, try responding with a statement rather than a question now and then.

I will show you a simple trick! These yes/no questions (sometimes known as the gradual death of a conversation) are easy to ask:

"Did you enjoy yourself?"

"Did that make you nervous?"

Simply make an educated guess and turn those questions into statements:

"It appears you enjoy it!"

"That stressed you out."

You can avoid the interview vibe by rephrasing your questions as statements, and it will make the other person feel much more relaxed. Even better is that you will make the other person feel understood, giving the sense that you two are really connected!

And do not worry if you guess incorrectly. The person will simply correct you and continue with their story.

- **Observe and Compliment**

As you talk to someone, take note of the logo on their T-shirt, jewelry, sense of humor, overall energy level, and expressions. Acknowledge what you love about them to make your friend feel appreciated and seen.

People enjoy talking about themselves when given the opportunity, and they also enjoy receiving compliments. Finding anything to compliment, whether it is their clothing or something more personal, can help them open up to you more because they feel safe and appreciated. Compliments might also spark a conversation. For example, you could say, "I'm so curious where you got that fabulous bag" if you want to use the compliment to start a conversation.

- **Use Their Name Often**

The sound of your name can feel really soothing. It is too bad we don't hear it more frequently!

So, let's make a change. Drop the other person's name every couple of phrases. Drop it at the start of a statement or at the end of a question!

Right after they tell you their name, do this:

"My name is Michael. What is your name?"

"I'm Josh."

"It's great to finally meet you, Josh!"

"So, Josh, what do you think about . . .?" a minute later.

It is a two-for-one deal. It not only makes the other person feel more at ease, but it also makes it much simpler for you to recall their name the next time you meet.

- **Use the Ford Rule**

Talk about your family, job, hobbies, and dreams. These are safe themes that can be used in many different ways.

Family, recreation, and occupation are topics of small talk I like to use when I'm feeling anxious. Conversations about interests, passions, and dreams are the most interesting. However, small talk is required before individuals feel comfortable diving further into more exciting issues.

- **Master Talking over Text**

Texting is not for everyone, and it is easy to get caught up in the details of brief and delayed responses. Whoever you are texting could potentially be preoccupied and not in a position to interact with their smartphone fully. You can always ask if it is a good time or if they would prefer to call or meet up in person.

Do not take it personally if someone responds with one-word answers. Instead, continue to pay attention to them. Remember that communicating over text is much different than in person, so short responses don't always mean they are annoyed or don't want to talk to you.

If you wish to send your message clearly and directly, using an emoji is one way to do so. This can work well in a text conversation because it allows you to show emotion with a form of communication that primarily relies on words to send a message.

Be straightforward. One disadvantage of texting is the possibility of things getting lost in translation. Because you can't show body language in a text, it's important to use your words to fill in those blanks. For example, you might say, "I have been thinking about you and hoping to hear from you. I would be happy to hear anything you have to say!"

- **If You Don't Know, Say You Don't Know**

Lying is one of the most common mistakes people make during conversations because it makes them appear unpredictable and untrustworthy.

Others value vulnerability and honesty, and they should always be present in a positive social interaction. Understand that it is totally acceptable not to know everything and that no one expects you to.

- **Ask for Their Opinion**

Don't you just adore it when someone thinks so highly of you that they seek your opinion on something? It is, without a doubt, the best. Asking for your friend's opinion makes them feel valued.

You do not have to ask about anything life-changing. Instead, you could simply ask, "Can I get your opinion on . . .?"

"I would like to try a few of the restaurants in this area. Actually, may I get your opinion on it? Do you have a favorite restaurant here?"

- **Use Storytelling**

Everyone understands that stories brighten up conversations, yet most people only share personal stories. When talking to someone, you don't have to use stories from your life only. You can use stories from anywhere you want. It could be stories about people you know to stories you heard on the TV, radio, or in a magazine article.

How will you weave the stories into your discussion?

Try to think of a story from something you've read that relates to what you're talking about. For instance, if you're studying with a classmate from your English class about an upcoming test on Shakespeare, you can mention an interesting fact you found out about him from an article you read.

- **Look for Silent Registry**

Silent registry is when a person appears to stop and think about what is said. That is frequently where the person(s) is engaged because something you said has struck a chord, and they are thinking about how to respond.

Do not use silence to irritate the other person, though. If the conversation becomes too difficult to handle at this point, explain why you are hesitant to speak, then end the conversation.

- **Handle Heated Discussions Well**

There are several ways to exit an argument gracefully. Here are four easy statements that will end an argument 99 percent of the time.

- **"Let me think about it."**

This statement works because it buys you time to think about your response. When you argue, your body prepares for a fight by increasing your heart rate and blood pressure, and you might even sweat. This response is known as your fight-or-flight mode. Your mental focus narrows, and you become preoccupied with the danger in front of you. As a result, your problem-solving skills suffer. Allowing yourself to think gives your body an opportunity to relax. This mental pause also sends a message to the other party that you care enough to consider their point of view, which reassures them you care about their feelings.

- **"I understand."**

These words are effective because they help you show empathy toward your friend. When you say these words, you change the direction of an argument because seeking to understand someone else's point of view is not an argument. These words can be difficult to say since pausing to understand can feel like giving up on the conversation. You should also note that showing understanding doesn't mean you agree with them. It simply means you respect them enough to acknowledge their feelings.

- **"You could be right."**

This statement is effective because it shows a willingness to compromise. Most people will soften their response when they hear this statement, and they will take a step back as well.

You do not have to believe the other person is correct. You simply accept that their point of view may have merit and hint that you will think about what they have said. It can often disarm someone if they feel the conversation heading into a more heated disagreement.

- **"I'm sorry."**

These are really powerful words in the English language. Unfortunately, most of us are hesitant to apologize because we think it implies admitting guilt and accepting full responsibility. Unfortunately, this viewpoint frequently makes the problem worse. Apologies change the narrative from "it's not my fault" to "I understand."

- **Learn to Be Okay with Silence**

Conversations naturally include silence. The silence is only uncomfortable if you panic and make it so.

When there is an awkward silence, it doesn't mean you are the only one who needs to come up with something to say. A socially savvy friend once taught me this lesson. The other person is undoubtedly under the same strain. At times, practice being comfortable with silence. You will help the other person relax if you continue the discussion in a relaxed manner rather than stressing out while trying to think of something to say.

- **Do Not Allow Interruptions**

Interrupters do so for many reasons, just a few of which add value or enhance the conversation. Some people interrupt because they do not pay attention. Others might interrupt because they do not respect you or the other people in the conversation. When there is little to no respect, it is difficult to have a mutually beneficial conversation. Finally, some people interrupt because they believe they have something exciting or important to say.

If the other person keeps interrupting, you can end the conversation and walk away. However, don't feel the need to continue the conversation just to be courteous. Ending the conversation can help you set a healthy boundary in your social interactions that favors respectful conversations.

- **Be Positive**

If you insult someone else's interests, they will most likely avoid speaking with you, making the interaction unpleasant. Try the following instead of criticizing:

Ask why the person is so enthusiastic about their pastime. There could be more to their fascination than you realize.

Put some effort into discovering some common ground. Building this connection will help you understand their viewpoint better. For example, if someone talks about their passion for horseback riding and you find it uninteresting, you could extend the conversation to include all outdoor activities. You could then discuss nature, fitness, or riding your bike.

- **Keeping the Conversation Going Online**

Send a photo of something strange or amusing you saw, a song you enjoy, or an article that reminded you of the other person. Tell them what you think and seek their feedback. Just like shared activities can stimulate conversations in person, the same is true for online engagement. You could also, for example, watch a movie together, take the same personality test, explore a museum virtually, or listen to the same playlist.

These suggestions will help you keep the conversation alive and make it enjoyable. The next chapter is devoted to maintaining a connection with people and gaining insight into meaningful relationships.

Chapter Takeaway:

- Be mindful of your tone of voice, listening skills, and body language.
- Be honest, assertive, and use valuable tips to keep the conversation fun and interesting.

four
the art of maintaining connection

> 66 When we seek for connection, we restore the world to wholeness.

MARGARET J. WHEATLEY

DUNBAR'S NUMBER Theory says we can maintain 150 stable relationships.[1]

Just for fun, what number do you want? How many meaningful relationships do you have?

This chapter will explore meaningful relationships in detail, from the *what* to the *how* of relationships. So, let's get into it.

4.1 Finding Meaning in Relationships

Have you ever felt lonely, even in a room full of people? This might sound odd, but I am sure you have experienced this. I have too. It amazes me how lonely we can feel even in the closest relationships, especially when we don't feel understood.

Loneliness is not defined by the number of people around us or the number of days we spend with them. Many of us are always on the lookout for affection and acceptance. We are under the impression that we must change or conform. Still, we only experience emotional death when we attempt to fit in rather than being accepted unconditionally as we are. Loneliness can be defined as a perceived lack of quality in our relationships with others, but it stems from a fundamental need for acceptance that we all share.

Is not loneliness a scream for real connection, a kind of bond with another human being that allows us to share our hearts openly while being welcomed and loved by the person on the other end? Many of us might be unsure how to form these deep bonds with others. Finding people who want to have a deep conversation can be difficult, even for those of us who are good at making meaningful connections. Finding someone to spend quality time with is challenging and requires you to make the first painfully vulnerable step.

What Does a Meaningful Connection Feel Like?

Forming meaningful connections requires a great deal of vulnerability. You must be honest with your peers, giving them affection and receiving it in return. We also value forming meaningful connections with someone we can trust. When we need to share or get support, they show up for us—and we show up for them. These meaningful connections ask us to be selfless because it's about more than simply meeting our needs. You likely have many of these relationships right now with family members, friends, neighbors, or romantic partners if you've started dating.

If you are worried or unhappy, you look to these people to brighten your day. They are also the people you first think of when you have exciting news to share, like an excellent grade on a test or getting a new after-school job.

The friend who contacts you when they need to vent is a meaningful connection. And you eagerly accept the call because you are interested in hearing what they have to say. This is the same person you would be thrilled for if they called to tell you something wonderful had happened in their lives. You are concerned for their well-being, whether it is good news or bad.

Here are some examples to clarify what meaningful connections do not entail.

Connecting with individuals on Facebook, LinkedIn, Instagram, and Twitter—where you can see what they are up to, learn about their lifestyle, and follow their "likes" and posts—doesn't show a genuine connection.

Finding a mentor at work who opens doors for you is a great thing to find, but this is not a meaningful connection

Qualities of a Meaningful Connection

These seven essential elements must be present in meaningful relationships:

- **Communication** is the act of expressing and receiving another person's thoughts, ideas, and feelings. It is vital to relationships because it is the only way we have to connect. It is crucial to the other qualities listed below, and it is usually the first thing to go when a relationship starts to fall apart.
- **Honesty** means that your words and actions say the same thing. It is the key to building trust. Without it, the connection is likely to fail. Expressing clear expectations of yourself and the other person, admitting any mistakes, and expressing how you truly feel are all examples of being honest.
- **Respect** is holding someone else, their ideas, and their existence in high regard and in a favorable light. In a respectful connection, you take time to show the other person you value who they are and what they bring to the friendship.

- **Dependability** means you do what you say you will do consistently. When you find this quality in a friend, you know you'll always be able to count on them to show up for you.
- **Interdependence** is when two independent people join forces to form a strong bond. This quality is evident in relationships that benefit both people because you make the other's life better by being in it.
- **Empathy** exists when you consider another person's ideas, feelings, and emotions. When you show empathy for another person, you focus on fully understanding the other person's feelings.
- Every strong connection has a reason for its existence—a reason for two people to connect. Without a significant reason to form a bond, a relationship is not worth the time or effort because at least one of the participants sees no value in it.

Mirror Neurons and Human Connection

Making meaningful connections is necessary for you to reach your greatest potential. How our brains build human connections is the subject of a growing body of knowledge.

Mirror neurons reflect an action we see in someone else, causing us to mimic it or feel compelled to do so. These do-it-yourself neurons provide a brain mechanism that explains the adage, "When you smile, the whole world smiles with you."

Your social environment significantly impacts how you experience joy throughout your life, now and in the future. Not only do these connections make us feel less lonely, but they also contribute to an overall sense of well-being.

Think about how it feels when you see someone struggle with the same things you do. It creates an immediate connection in your brain, essentially telling you that you're not alone. Your human need for connection often takes this recognition a bit further by compelling you to form a bond with this person because you understand each other.

What Might Be Stopping Me from Having a Meaningful Connection?

The emphasis on being self-sufficient might be one explanation for the decline in social connection. When you learn to rely only on yourself, you trick yourself into thinking you don't need to connect with others to survive. Communities can dissolve when we believe they add no value to our lives. Friendships decline as a result, and our neighbors become complete strangers. This disconnect turns self-sufficiency —which is supposed to be a positive quality— into a weakness because there are no meaningful relationships to enhance your life.

Another factor contributing to the recent drop in good, meaningful relationships is that we are too distracted by technology, especially cell phones. Think about how often you check your phone for a text message or a social media notification. It's a lot more often than you think! We are always in a different world when we are distracted by digital devices, making authentic and meaningful conversation difficult. While cell phones allow us to stay in touch with people who are not physically there, they also make it difficult to connect with those who are.

Perhaps these factors play a role in pulling us apart. But, whatever the cause, increased loneliness and a lack of supportive relationships are harmful to our health.

4.2 My Relationship Skills

Though technology was created to improve our lives, it turns out that it also hurts us at the same time. The ability to connect more digitally has driven us apart relationally. You might have 1,000 friends on Facebook, but how many of them have resulted in genuine connections? This distinction often results in us feeling more alone than ever.

Nobody benefits from being alone. Here are some tips for making any relationship more meaningful:

- **Keep Connection Building in Mind**

Two people form a connection when they share an emotional experience. When you talk to someone, they tell you about their life, and you tell them about your life. Find out what you two have in common, your shared passions, and what you want from life. You'll likely find something in this relationship that strengthens and supports your life in some way as you continue to explore what you have in common.

- **Avoid Superficial Conversations**

It is very easy to feel connected in today's world. We can text each other several times a day, check each other's Instagram feeds, and even speak with each other while enjoying an online game. We might think we know what is happening in each other's life. It is not the reality, however, because it only results in a one-dimensional connection.

- **Value Quality over Quantity**

When it comes to developing strong, honest relationships, less is more. Making a meaningful relationship requires effort. Your eyes might glaze over just thinking about the number of responsibilities on your plate. Understandably, finding time to spend with a large group of friends can seem overwhelming. However, developing a stronger bond with two or three close buddies is significantly more manageable.

It is not necessary to be in a crowd to feel connected. A low-pressure, high-quality shared experience can be had by spending valuable time with a few people you connect deeper with rather than ten acquaintances. Choose face-to-face connections and engage in activities together, such as hiking, studying, or watching a movie.

- ## **Understand That We Are All Different**

Everyone in your life comes with unique experiences and opinions you might not have been exposed to otherwise. This uniqueness can contribute to your happiness by making you more diverse and educated. What you learn can also be shared with others throughout your life to make their lives more meaningful.

- ## **Reach Out**

Reaching out is the first and sometimes most difficult step. Why? Because you put yourself out there every time you attempt to connect with another person.

Pursuing these connections enhances your life more than simply waiting for them to find you. You do this by initiating conversations and staying in touch. Since life can be hectic, make time for connecting throughout your day.

Regardless of how you met—at school, on the soccer field, or in your neighborhood—to progress to friendship, you must extend an invitation.

Have faith in your vulnerability and courage. Take the initiative. Make an effort to connect.

- **Use Eye Contact**

Eye contact is quite effective. Looking someone in the eyes creates a social connection. A connected gaze fosters empathy and demonstrates that we are aware of and paying attention to the other person.

Our eyes even blink in sync when we make deep eye contact. We share feelings and intentions.

As you communicate and share, allow your eyes to keep steady eye contact. Relax your eyes so it doesn't make them feel like you are staring at them. The eyes are appropriately referred to as the "windows to the soul." Use intense eye contact to help you understand and see the person in front of you when looking for a deeper connection.

- **Be Yourself**

Genuine connection comes from letting your guard down and allowing your true self to shine through. This self-expression can be really difficult for many people. However, being genuine means we also need to be vulnerable. We must express our true selves, leaving us vulnerable to emotional pain, rejection, and judgment.

Many of us are envious of others, thinking, *If only I had their money, if only I had their looks*, or *if only I were more popular*. But we do not understand that by trying to be someone else, we are like a round peg trying to fit into a square hole because we assume that having this one thing will make us happy. Embrace your uniqueness and let it shine.

Use the suggestions below to help you overcome any reservations you might have about authenticity:

- **Strive for Self-Awareness:** Recognize what you feel when you try to shut people out. Consider what is stopping you from opening up. Allow yourself to investigate and become aware of the triggers that force you to conceal your true nature.
- **Give Your Fears a Voice:** Begin by being open and honest with the people closest to you. Give a voice to the things that

prevent you from opening up. Many of us have similar thoughts about vulnerability, and you will probably find that your closest friends have similar fears.

- **Do Not Put Too Much Pressure on Yourself:** Do not put yourself under undue strain to achieve perfection. It should not be your goal in life to please everyone you meet. That is impossible. You don't need others to validate your identity. Trying to please others at the expense of your authenticity leads to disappointment, sadness, and anger. And do you really want to waste your time with a group of people who have no idea who you are?

- **Remember You Are Special**

You have a unique collection of experiences, just like others do. And once you connect with your core self, accept who you are and feel at ease in your own skin. You will recognize that you are a unique individual with a lot to offer the world that few others can. You can focus on using what you have to create something brilliant for the world that no one else could possibly produce.

- **Dive Deeper**

You must engage in small talk for a while before asking others deeper questions. We must go beneath the surface to get to know someone. Deep questions shift your conversation away from pleasantries and small talk and into intimacy and vulnerability. We get to know someone there.

Psychology professor Dan McAdams identifies three levels of knowing someone that typically lead to deeper friendships:[2]

- **General characteristics:** Characteristics, personality, quirks, and tendencies.
- **Personal concerns:** Beliefs, worldview, values, and philosophy.
- **Self-narrative:** The stories we tell about ourselves, how we see the world and life, and how we find meaning and purpose.

- **Keep Your Commitments**

Trust is the foundation of deep and meaningful relationships. Breaching commitments is one of the surest ways to destroy trust. If you consistently break promises, your reputation and relationships will suffer.

Avoid the temptation to overcommit to your promises. It is better to say no than to commit and back out later. Consider your motivations if you frequently fall into the over-commitment trap: Is it difficult to set limits by saying "no"? Do you dislike disappointing others and genuinely desire to help but lack the necessary resources? Have you ever said "yes" on the spur of the moment, only to regret it later? Here are some suggestions for managing commitments:

- **Write It in Your Calendar:** If it isn't on your calendar, it isn't going to happen. So, to avoid being neglected or forgotten, plan your commitments as soon as you make them.
- **Stop the Commitment/Cancellation Cycle:** You can stop this cycle by delaying your response when asked for a favor. Instead, request time to look at your calendar and ensure you can meet the deadline. Then promise to respond

with a solid answer within twenty-four hours—and stick to it.

- **Do It Even If You Do Not Feel Like It:** For example, you are not in the mood to focus on history when your study date arrives. Do it anyway. Be present for people once you have committed because they are counting on you to deliver. Consider how you would feel if your friends abandoned you in a similar situation. A meaningful connection is founded on trust, and part of that trust is earned through consistency and reliability.

- **Leave Something Good Behind**

You want to move into this world, express your uniqueness, learn, mature, and engage with that unique experience to make something that will have an impact long after you are gone. Make it your top priority to figure out how you can do something that will transform the lives of hundreds of people because what you leave behind is the only thing that will remain when you are gone.

- **Follow Up**

Follow-up is the most basic yet overlooked activity in developing solid relationships.

Following up with someone can take many different forms, such as:

- After you have done something together, send a text message that shows your gratitude for the experience.
- Remember a key event or date for the other person and wish them well.
- Ask about major events in a person's life, both positive and negative.
- Thank someone for something they did for you, their commitment to the friendship, or their contribution to your life.

We are human, and no matter how much we try to convince ourselves that "I can handle this on my own," we know we require genuine connection and a sense of belonging.

We naturally feel valued when someone follows up with us.

On the other hand, following up does not require much effort. Remind yourself of all the good feelings you get when someone writes you a follow-up note and do it for them.

The more real ways you follow up, the faster you will develop a meaningful relationship.

- **Accept Feedback**

Accepting honest comments and constructive criticism is part of forming deep connections. It helps to have a helpful ally in your corner when communicating with friends. A good friend will also help you look at all sides of an issue objectively, often revealing a viewpoint you hadn't considered.

Maintain eye contact and be attentive to your body language to show you're open to input (for example, stern facial expressions and crossed arms can signal resistance to feedback). Refrain from defending yourself or interrupting. Accept feedback with an open mind and express gratitude to the speaker for expressing their honest thoughts. Take time to consider what you have heard and how you can use it.

- **Mix it Up**

Keep your relationships fresh and secure by changing things up, adding to your routine, setting goals, or trying new things. You might add excitement to your relationship and strengthen your bond by trying new things together.

You must constantly make fresh memories together to build lasting connections.

Suppose Bertha and Edna have played checkers weekly for the past two years. They may have a good routine, ask each other questions, and keep track of one other's life. However, the conversations will eventually follow a similar pattern, making the friendship feel much too routine.

They might have a fresh common experience and something to talk about if they did something different like playing chess.

We allow ourselves to mature as a person and share that progress with each other by switching things up. This change in our routine improves our bond with the other person through this process of growth and introspection.

Take an inventory of the relationships you already have and come up with new activities and ideas. If the people in your life also yearn for a deeper connection, they will likely leap at the chance to shake things up.

• Do Not Control Anyone

We often say, "If she did this, she wouldn't be so unhappy," or "if he did this, I would be happy." But the reality is that you can only move yourself; you cannot control other people's behavior, and you cannot expect other people to do things merely to make you happy. If you feel unsatisfied on the inside, nothing on the outside will make you feel otherwise.

• Do Not Force Anything

This lesson is something I am extremely enthusiastic about, and I understand that it can be difficult to accept when things appear to be at their worst. However, the truth is that we can't see the big picture of how everything will turn out, and we can't honestly know whether a situation was bad or good until we find out where it takes us eventually.

Building meaningful relationships can be difficult, and you may feel as if those around you don't understand you or are unwilling to show up for you. I understand, and I will tell you this: You deserve connection. You are deserving of recognition. You will find people who have the ability and want to form lasting relationships, so keep looking if you have not already. Because they are worth it, and you are too.

Chapter Takeaway:

- Make sure you understand what meaningful relationships mean.
- Building a meaningful relationship with someone requires time and effort.
- You need to be vulnerable and respect each other's differences to connect with someone.

afterword

The quality of our relationships influences our emotional, physical, and mental well-being greatly. Relationships take various shapes, from family and friends to romantic partners and mentors. Finally, the value of our relationships is subjective and varies from person to person.

Although there isn't one definition of meaningfulness, many of us value similar approaches to expanding our relationships, finding meaning and purpose, and learning to establish and experience authentic connections.

For instance, social media allows us to communicate with a lot of other people. When a screen controls those connections, the joy you derive from them is diminished. It is nice to get likes from friends and fans, but virtual hugs don't compare to the real thing. Digital relationships do not entirely scratch the itch for meaningful encounters that we all experience. Engagement, empathy, and exchanges that enhance your bond are necessary to form a meaningful connection with another person. Breaking through superficial barriers and growing together through life's ups and downs requires genuine attention and effort.

Positive Social Skills for Teens is a guidebook to help teens improve their relationships and ability to interact with people.

The first chapter focused on assisting teens in exploring and understanding themselves so they know what they bring to the table for others and what kind of relationships they want. Some strategies include journaling, evaluating their strengths and weaknesses, figuring out their values, understanding their priorities, observing their behavior, and realizing what makes them happy and resonates with them. The chapter also discusses the importance of relationships in a person's life.

The second chapter is devoted to explaining strategies for building confidence. This exploration includes accepting your personality, understanding why you need confidence, preparing yourself, not letting negative thoughts impact you, putting your beliefs to the test, expecting the unexpected, being mindful of your tone of voice and body language, and remembering who you are and what you value. It also includes strategies to help you if you feel like you do not belong and would not fit in no matter what you did.

The third chapter is about strategies to engage in effective communication. It moves from general to specific tips about handling a conversation. This exploration includes active listening, avoiding judgment, expressing yourself clearly, going with the flow, managing your emotions, clarifying what you heard, using manners, using the Ford method, finding common ground, and learning to be okay with silence.

The fourth chapter revolves around building and maintaining meaningful relationships. It discusses the concept, qualities, psychology, and barriers to relationships. The chapter ends with strategies, such as avoiding superficial conversations, preferring quality over quantity, understanding we are all different, reaching out to others, keeping your commitments, leaving something good behind, and following up.

We are born to add spark to each other's lives. If you think this book helped you do that, it would mean a lot to me if you could leave an honest review. Feedback is the best way to learn how I can improve and provide more value to you in the future.

Thank you for your support!

I am on Instagram at:

@victoria.day_author

references

Introduction

1. Admiral William H. McRaven, "Make Your Bed,"(speech, University of Texas at Austin, May 17, 2014), James Clear, https://jamesclear.com/great-speeches/make-your-bed-by-admiral-william-h-mcraven.
2. Dr. Saul McLeod, "Maslow's Hierarchy of Needs," *Simply Psychology*, April 4, 2022, https://www.simplypsychology.org/maslow.html.

1. The Art of Exploring Yourself

1. Carnegie Mellon University, "Stress on Disease," April 2, 2012, https://www.cmu.edu/homepage/health/2012/spring/stress-on-disease.shtml.
2. G. Oscar Anderson, "Loneliness and Social Connections: A National Survey of Adults 45 and Older," *AARP®*, September 2018, https://www.aarp.org/research/topics/life/info-2018/loneliness-social-connections.html.
3. J.H. Fowler and N.A. Christakis, "Dynamic Spread of Happiness in a Large Social Network: Longitudinal Analysis over 20 Years in the Framingham Heart Study," *BMJ, 337*, no. dec04 2 (2008), https://doi.org/10.1136/bmj.a2338.
4. Jeff Haden, "A study of 300,000 people found living a longer, happier life isn't just about diet, exercise, or genetics," *Business Insider*, October 21, 2017, https://www.businessinsider.com/a-study-of-300000-people-reveals-the-keys-to-a-longer-happier-life-2017-10.

5. University of Chicago, "Feeling lonely adds to rate of blood pressure increase in people 50 years and older," *UChicago News*, March 17, 2010, https://news.uchicago.edu/story/feeling-lonely-adds-rate-blood-pressure-increase-people-50-years-old-and-older.

6. Margarita Tartakovsky, MS, "How to Know Yourself Better," *PsychCentral*, August 18, 2021, https://psychcentral.com/health/ways-to-get-to-know-yourself-better.

7. Ibid.

2. The Art of Being Confident

1. Kristen Baker, "The Ultimate Guide to Confidence," Hubspot, August 13, 2018, https://blog.hubspot.com/marketing/confidence.

4. The Art of Maintaining Connection

1. Jenny Gross, "Can You Have More Than 150 Friends?", *The New York Times*, May 11, 2021, https://www.nytimes.com/2021/05/11/science/dunbars-number-debunked.html.

2. John D. Mayer, Ph.D., "Three Levels of Knowing a Person," *Psychology Today*, November 8, 2010, https://www.psychologytoday.com/us/blog/the-personality-analyst/201011/three-levels-knowing-person.

Made in United States
North Haven, CT
21 February 2023

32966381R00074